CHRISTMAS MAKE & DO

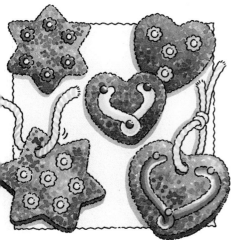

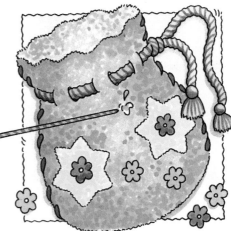

Gillian Chapman

Craft ideas which
bring the story of
Christmas to life

HOW TO USE THIS BOOK

You will find within this book a wealth of ideas and inspiration for using with your child, group or Key Stage 2 classes.

Discover fresh ideas for Christmas preparation and bring alive the New Testament accounts of the Nativity.

Craft ideas vary from the very simple to the more challenging, but the emphasis is strongly on using inexpensive materials and equipment, recycling and using domestic materials where possible. Children will experience the thrill of making something wonderful almost 'out of nothing'.

To help keep preparation time to a minimum, each project spread features:

✳ a lively retelling of the Bible story, suitable for reading aloud to a group

✳ a list of materials needed

✳ clear step-by-step instructions

✳ a photograph of how the finished article may look, in case you haven't had time to make one earlier!

All the craft ideas have been designed, tried and tested by Gillian Chapman, a well-known author of craft books.

Drawing on her wide experience of leading children's workshops on arts and crafts, she has prepared a helpful section of Bible Craft Tips and safety recommendations. It is worth taking a few moments to read through this section before you begin.

Part of the excitement and satisfaction of *Make and Do* crafts begins when children are able to develop their own original slant on an idea or design, whatever the results! Some children (and adults, let's face it) may struggle to follow instructions and lose interest very quickly if they feel an activity is too difficult. Bearing that in mind, most of the ideas in this book can be modified according to a child's ability. For example, where sewing is involved, you may use PVA glue instead; where drawing is involved, you may cut pictures out of magazines.

You will find clear photocopiable tracing guides and templates in the middle of this book as a helpful starting-point. Some of these could be enlarged to produce wall-sized pictures, collages or displays for bedrooms, classrooms or churches.

Specific projects, such as the Christmas bells and masks, could be used as props for drama productions. Having read the story and made the articles, children can enjoy the further dimension of bringing a story to life themselves through drama or dance.

There are endless possibilities for using *Christmas Make and Do* to explore the Bible. Enjoy them!

CONTENTS

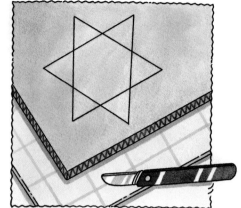

BIBLE CRAFT TIPS
Additional practical information

Shaped Scissors

Special scissors with a shaped cutting blade are increasingly available for craftwork. Use these, or pinking shears, to give paper and fabric a special patterned edge. You might need special scissors for the masks on pages 28-29.

Safety First

All tools and equipment must be used with care and respect! Sharp pencils, scissors and needles can all be dangerous if used incorrectly.

However, an adult will need to help with carpentry tools and cutting tools.

If you need to use a craft knife make sure you also use a cutting board.

Paints

Poster paints are great for painting on paper and card, also to paint models made from paper pulp and papier-mâché. They also come in metallic colours. Acrylic paints are better to paint wooden surfaces.

A jar of clean water will be needed to mix paints and to clean brushes. Change the water frequently to keep colours looking bright. Paints can be mixed on a palette or an old plate.

For detailed drawing of animals, figures and faces (as in the angel, shepherd and sheep decorations on pages 14-15) sketch in the outlines first with pencil, then colour in using coloured pencils. If you have a set of watercolour paints and a fine brush, use these.

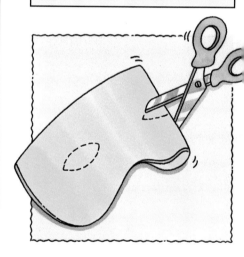

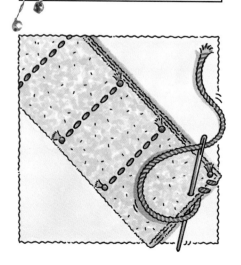

Glues

PVA glue is perfect for most craftwork. It can be diluted for papier mâché type projects. It will stick paper, card and most fabrics – but in most cases it must be used very sparingly. It will wash off with cold water while still wet.

Glue sticks are better for neat finishes, but only work on paper and thin card.

When using PVA to do fine work such as gluing beads and sequins on to fabric, try to buy the glue in a bottle with a fine nozzle. If you don't have such a container, then pour some of the glue into a small plastic container (like a lid) and use a cocktail stick to put tiny blobs of glue where it's needed. You will need to do this for the gift bags, finger puppets and face masks.

Brushes

Keep separate brushes for painting and gluing. Always clean them in warm soapy water after use and dry them before putting them away.

Keeping Clean

Make sure all work surfaces are protected with newspaper and all clothing is covered with overalls (e.g. an old shirt) or an apron. Keep an old towel handy for drying not-so-clean hands.

General tip for Christmas crafts

You can find all kinds of sparkly bits and pieces in stationers and arts and crafts shops, and they're all great to use for Christmas crafts. Look out for sparkly pipe cleaners, pom-poms, feathers, stars, all kinds of stickers, sequins, stick-on gems, ribbons, glitter glue, gold and silver pens.

Patterned and holographic card and paper comes in A4 packs, and you can buy card with all types of special finishes and effects.

Small Christmas decorations can also be used to decorate projects, small bits of tinsel and, of course, wrapping paper.

AN ANGEL VISITS MARY

News of the baby king!

Mary lived in a little town called Nazareth. She was soon to be married to Joseph, the carpenter. But one day she had a visitor with some surprising news which changed Mary's life for ever.

God sent the angel Gabriel to talk to Mary!

'Greetings!' said the angel. 'Don't be afraid. God has chosen you out of all the women in the world. You will have a baby and he will be called God's son. You shall call him Jesus. He will be a king for ever.'

'I am God's servant,' said Mary. 'I will do as God asks.'

The angel left, and Mary sang a song of praise to God for choosing her to be the mother of God's son.

Make this pop-up card as a reminder of Mary's surprise visit from the angel Gabriel.

You will need:

✂

A4 coloured card

Glue stick

Ruler, pencil and scissors

Paints and brush

Coloured stickers
or
holographic paper for decorating the card

Small length of gold cord and thread

1 Cut the A4 card in half. Fold one piece in half to make the card. It is easier to decorate the card before sticking in the pop-up, so paint a design on the back and front, or use coloured stickers if you have them.

2 Use the pencil and ruler to draw a strip 15cm x 3cm long on the second piece of card, then cut it out. Fold the strip exactly in half and crease the centre fold. Make two more folds in the strip 2cm from each end as shown. You can find tracing guides to help you on page 16.

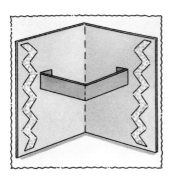

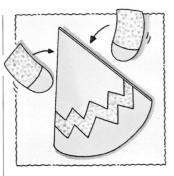

3 Place the strip in the middle of the card so that the creases in the strip and the card match exactly. Keep the strip in this position and stick the two ends to the card with the glue stick.

4 Either paint your pop-up angel or make it from scraps of paper as shown here. Cut out a triangular shape and two arms from the scraps of card you have left. Cover these with small pieces of holographic paper to decorate the angel's robes and glue the arms to the body.

5 Cut out two wings from holographic paper and an oval shape from plain card for the face. Draw the angel's face on to the oval and glue it to the top of the body. Glue the wings to the back. To make the curly hair take a 10cm piece of gold cord. Tie it firmly in the centre with thread and fray the ends, then glue the hair to the head.

6 When the glue is completely dry, fold the angel in half and make a firm crease along the centre fold. Glue the angel to the pop-up strip, making sure the crease on the strip and the angel's centre fold match up exactly. When you open the card, the angel will pop out.

MARY AND JOSEPH TRAVEL TO BETHLEHEM

At last they could see the rooftops of Bethlehem!

1 Make the pockets by folding one of the long strips of felt in half lengthways and pinning together. Mark out 12 pockets by drawing a line with the felt tipped pen at 5cm intervals along the strip.

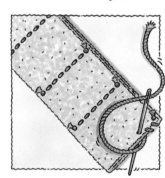

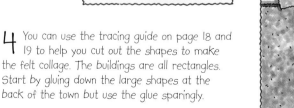

You will need:

60cm x 40cm piece of blue felt

Pins, needle and thread

2 strips of coloured felt, 60cm x 10cm

Scissors

Pieces of coloured felt: yellow, green, brown, grey, purple, etc.

PVA glue and spreader

Gold fabric marker pen

Ruler

Coloured braid and sequins for decoration (optional)

Fine felt tipped pen

24 small toys and sweets for the pockets

4 curtain rings

2 Sew along each line with a simple running stitch, knotting the thread at each end on the same side as the felt-tipped pen lines, making this side the back. Oversew each end of the strip. Repeat with the other strip until all 24 pockets are done.

3 Spread PVA glue along the back of the first strip of pockets and glue it to the bottom of the piece of blue felt. Then glue the second strip of pockets above the first. This leaves plenty of space above the pockets for the Bethlehem scene.

4 You can use the tracing guide on page 18 and 19 to help you cut out the shapes to make the felt collage. The buildings are all rectangles. Start by gluing down the large shapes at the back of the town but use the glue sparingly.

Mary had to wait many months before her baby was ready to be born. During that time, the Roman emperor had ordered a census. Joseph was told that he must go to Bethlehem to be counted.

Mary and Joseph had to travel all the way to Bethlehem on foot. Their donkey carried their clothes, food and a bottle of water. It was a very long, dusty journey. Mary became very tired. She was nearly ready to have her baby and needed to rest often.

'Come on, Mary,' said Joseph gently. 'We will soon see Bethlehem in the distance.'

Suddenly, over the brow of a hill, they could see the rooftops and trees of the little town of Bethlehem. At last they were nearly there!

Count down the days before Christmas with this Advent calendar!

5 Build up the scene, working forward and overlapping the houses. Position the palm trees by gluing the trunks down first, then adding the leaves. Finally, cut out lots of small yellow and orange squares and rectangles to make the lighted windows and doors.

6 Use the gold fabric marker to write the numbers 1 to 24 on each pocket. Add extra decorations and sequins if you have them and sew the curtain rings along the top of the calendar. Here's the fun part! Fill up all the pockets with sweets and small toys and hang up the calendar ready for 1 December.

BETHLEHEM IS FULL

No room at the inn!

You will need:

Rectangles of fabric or felt, approx 26cm x 12cm

Scissors, needle, sewing thread and pins

PVA glue, brush and cocktail sticks as an alternative to sewing

Small scraps of coloured fabric or felt for decoration

Lengths of coloured cord, approx 60cm for each bag

Sequins for decoration

When Mary and Joseph finally arrived in Bethlehem, they were very tired. Mary was getting worried. Her baby was soon going to be born! They needed to find a place to sleep for the night.

Joseph carried their heavy bags and knocked on the door of the inn. But it was already full! So many people had come to Bethlehem to be counted, just like Joseph. Now where could they stay?

The innkeeper saw that Mary was soon going to have a baby. He took pity on her.

'I'm sorry there's no room in my inn,' he said. 'But you are welcome to sleep in the place behind the inn where the animals sleep. At least the straw is dry and you'll be safe for the night.'

'Thank you!' said Joseph. Mary and Joseph and their donkey followed the innkeeper behind the inn. At last Mary could lie down and rest.

1 Fold the rectangle of fabric in half and pin the sides together. Sew along the two sides using small stitches and leave the top open. Alternatively you can glue the two sides together with PVA.

3 Cut out squares from different coloured felt or fabric and glue them in patterns to both sides of the bag. Then sew or glue sequins on to the bag to complete the design.

4 To make the drawstring bag, use the tips of the scissors carefully to snip a row of holes in the bag 3cm from the top. Make the holes about 2cm apart and large enough to thread the cord through.

5 Take a 60cm length of cord, tie knots approximately 3cm from each end and thread the cord in and out through the row of holes in the bag.

2 To make the bag with the long cord strap, take the 60cm length of cord and tie a knot approximately 3cm from each end to stop the cord from fraying. Then sew (or glue) the cord along both sides of the bag so the knots are positioned in the two bottom corners of the bag.

6 Cut out some star shapes from coloured felt and glue them around the bag. Then sew or glue sequins on to the bag and around the opening. Fill the bags with sweets or small toys to make really special Christmas gifts.

Make these special gift bags and remember Mary and Joseph's journey to Bethlehem.

JESUS IS BORN

Mary has a baby boy

The time soon came for Mary's baby to be born.

'It's a boy!' shouted Joseph.

'He is called Jesus,' said Mary. The angel Gabriel had told her to give him that special name.

Mary looked lovingly at her tiny first-born son. He was so precious to her, and so helpless now. But Mary knew that God had a very important plan for his son. He would change the world.

Mary wrapped her baby in cloths and laid him in the soft hay in a manger to sleep.

Make these finger puppets to recreate the wonder of the Christmas story.

You will need:

✂

Scraps of coloured felt and fabric

Scissors and pins

Sewing needle and threads to match the felt

PVA glue, brush and cocktail sticks

Beads and scraps of yarn to decorate the figures

1 To make Joseph, the shepherds and wise men, use the templates on pages 16 and 17 as a guide to cut out all the felt pieces. You will need two body shapes, arms, head dress, face and beard for each puppet. Pin the two body pieces together and sew around the edge with small stitches, leaving the bottom open. (Alternatively the body pieces could be glued together.)

2 Glue the arms into position across the back. Use the cocktail stick to glue all the other small pieces of felt to the body, dabbing small amounts of PVA where it is needed.

3 The head dress is glued in place over the top of the body, then the face and beard. Finally glue the beads to the face, a small stick to a hand and a small piece of thread around the head as a headband. Use different coloured felt for all the men and decorate the wise men's clothes with beads and give them a gift to hold.

5 To make the animals, use the templates to cut out all the pieces of felt you need. Pin and sew the body pieces together as before. To make the sheep, sew the nose to the face shape and glue two ears to the back of the face, then glue the face to the body.

6 For the donkey and ox, glue their nose shapes, ears and eyes directly on to the bodies. Make their tails and manes from pieces of yarn which you can sew or glue in place.

4 To make Mary, follow the instructions for Joseph but use the needle and red thread to sew the nose and mouth features to the face before gluing the face over the head dress. To make baby Jesus, use the body shape, but cut 5mm off the length. Cut out and glue on a smaller face and sew two eyes as shown. Cut out a strip of grey felt long enough to wrap round the baby. Glue on, crossing it over the front of the body.

SHEPHERDS HEAR THE GOOD NEWS

A Saviour is born!

In the fields near Bethlehem, there were shepherds looking after their sheep. It was night and wild animals prowled around. The shepherds had to keep watch.

Suddenly the whole sky was filled with a dazzling light. The shepherds covered their eyes in fear.

'Don't be afraid!' said a voice. It was the angel of the Lord. 'I bring good news of great joy! Today in the town of Bethlehem a Saviour has been born to you. This will be a sign to you: you will find the baby wrapped in cloths and lying in a manger.'

Then a great host of angels appeared, singing beautiful songs to God:

'Glory to God in the highest, and peace on earth to all people!'

The angels went back to heaven. The shepherds watched in amazement.

You will need:

FOR THE SHEEP:

White felt and small scraps of grey felt

Cotton wool

White thread and sewing needle

Small beads for eyes

FOR THE ANGEL AND SHEPHERD:

Sheets of coloured paper

Small pieces of fabric and lace

Sticky tape

Felt tipped pens, stickers for decoration

Gold cord for angel's hair

FOR ALL DECORATIONS:

Gold Christmas thread, small gold bells

Scissors

PVA glue and cocktail sticks

1 To make the sheep, use the template on page 20 to draw two sheep shapes on to the white felt. Cut out a pale grey face, two dark grey felt ears and a nose. Pin the body shapes together and sew around the edge with small stitches, leave a small gap to pad the body with cotton wool, then sew up the gap.

2 Glue the two ears to the back of the face and glue the face to the body. Then glue the nose and two small bead eyes to the face.

3 Sew four lengths of gold thread to the body for legs. Thread a small bell to the end of each leg and secure with a knot. Also sew a loop of gold thread to the top of the sheep and use this to hang the sheep on the tree or a hook.

Make these decorations to remind you of the shepherds who heard about Jesus.

4 To make the angel, cut a semi-circular shape from the coloured paper, curl it into a cone shape and secure it with sticky tape. Also cut out the wing shapes, the arms and face from coloured paper.

5 Keeping the sticky tape at the back, glue the wings to the back of the cone and the arms to the front. Draw the angel's face with felt tipped pens and glue in place. Decorate the angel's dress with lace or coloured stickers. For hair, take a 10cm piece of gold cord. Tie it firmly in the centre with thread and fray the ends, then glue the hair to the head.

6 Stick two lengths of gold thread to the inside of the cone body with sticky tape. Make sure the gold threads are long enough to make the legs dangle below the body, then knot a small bell to each end. Stick a loop of gold thread to the back of the face with sticky tape and use this to hang the angel on the tree.

7 Make the shepherds in the same way but use different coloured papers decorated with felt tipped pens. Give them a head dress and a beard made from coloured paper instead of wings.

TRACING GUIDES

AN ANGEL VISITS MARY
Pages 6-7

JESUS IS BORN
Pages 12-13

Sheep

Cow

Donkey

Finger puppets - actual size

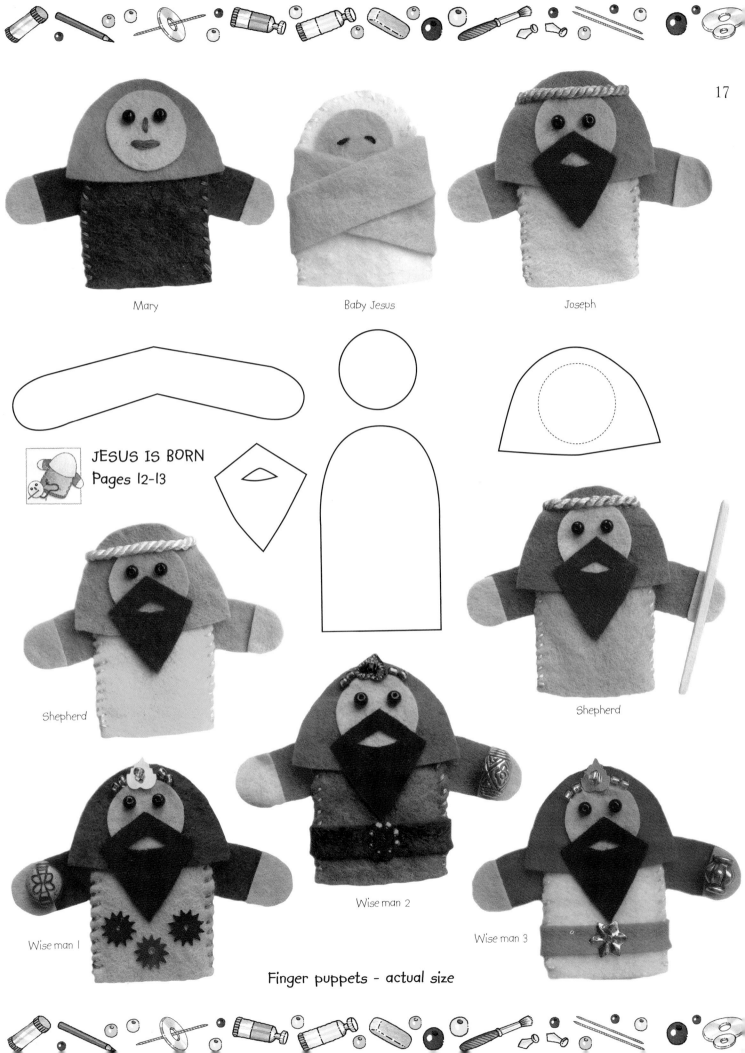

Mary

Baby Jesus

Joseph

JESUS IS BORN
Pages 12-13

Shepherd

Shepherd

Wise man 2

Wise man 1

Wise man 3

Finger puppets - actual size

TRACING GUIDES

MARY AND JOSEPH
TRAVEL TO BETHLEHEM
Pages 8-9

A NEW STAR IN THE SKY
Pages 26-27

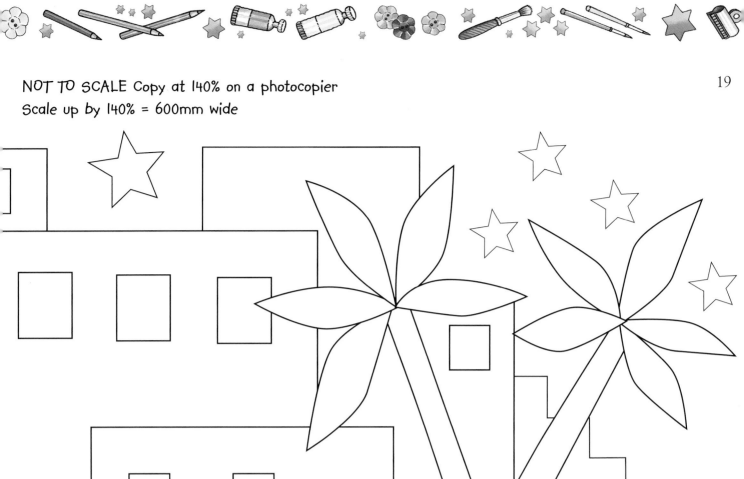

NOT TO SCALE Copy at 140% on a photocopier
Scale up by 140% = 600mm wide

TRACING GUIDES

SHEPHERDS HEAR
THE GOOD NEWS
Pages 14-15

22

SHEPHERDS GO TO FIND JESUS
The baby in the manger

'Hurry, hurry!' shouted the shepherds. 'We must hurry to Bethlehem at once to find the baby which God has told us about!'

They hurried through the town, looking for a new-born baby. They knocked at the door of an inn.

'Is there a baby here?' they asked the innkeeper.

The innkeeper showed the shepherds through to the back of the house, where the animals slept. And here they found Mary and Joseph. There, in a manger, wrapped up in cloths, was the new-born baby: Jesus, their Saviour. The shepherds looked at the tiny baby and they felt great joy in their hearts.

When they had said goodbye, they hurried into the town telling everyone they met, 'We've seen Jesus!'

They danced and sang songs to God, praising him for all they had seen. It had been just as the angel had said.

You will need:

✂

2 x 12cm lengths of thin card tube (fax rolls are ideal, but ask an adult to cut the lengths)

Scissors

4 x glittery coloured pipe cleaners

8 x bells

2 x pieces of Christmas wrapping paper 14cm x 14cm

Glue stick

PVA glue and brush

Lengths of pretty ribbon

Scraps of coloured tissue paper

1 Place the card tube on top of the wrapping paper, leaving 1cm of paper at either end. Use the glue stick to glue the paper to the tube and tuck the excess paper into the ends of the tube.

2 Twist two of the pipe cleaners together to join them and keep twisting for approximately 8cm. Then thread the first bell on to one pipe cleaner and twist the pipe cleaners together again to hold the bell in place.

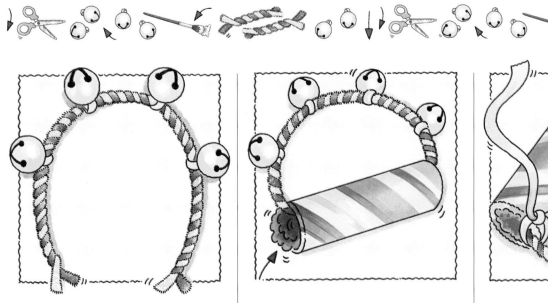

3 Continue twisting the pipe cleaners together, threading on all four bells at equal distances apart. Finish off twisting the last length of pipe cleaners together.

4 Dab a little PVA glue on to the ends of the pipe cleaners, covering about 5cm at both ends. Push the pipe cleaners into each end of the tube and leave to dry. If the card tube is rather wide, fill any gaps with scrunched up pieces of coloured paper. Dabs of glue will hold it in place.

5 Finally, tie a length of ribbon around the pipe cleaners at either end of the tube, just where they are attached to the tube. Repeat these instructions to make the second set of Christmas bells. Now sing like the shepherds!

Shake these Christmas bells to celebrate the good news that Jesus has been born.

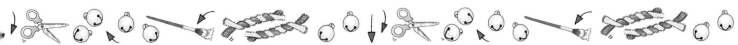

JESUS IS PRESENTED IN THE TEMPLE

A very special baby

When Jesus was eight days old, Mary and Joseph took him to the Temple in Jerusalem with two doves as their offering. They wanted to present him to God and say thank you for their new son.

In the Temple there was a very old man called Simeon. He had been waiting all his life to see the Saviour whom God had promised to send. God had told Simeon that he would not die until he had seen him.

When Mary and Joseph came near with Jesus, Simeon knew at once that this was the special child he had been waiting all his life to see. He took Jesus in his arms and thanked God.

'Lord God, now I may go in peace for I have seen the Saviour, the one who will bring light to all the people of God.'

Simeon blessed them. He knew that Jesus was a very special baby and would grow up to do great things.

You will need:

3 x long craft pipe cleaners

Kitchen towel

Sticky tape

Thick corrugated card

PVA glue and brush

Craft knife and cutting board

Gold poster paint and brush

Lid, approx 8cm diameter

Newspaper

Red candle and scraps of tinsel for decoration

Some adult help with using the craft knife and lighting the candle

SAFETY NOTE: This project is designed to be used as a Christmas table decoration. The candle should always be lit by an adult and should never be left unattended.

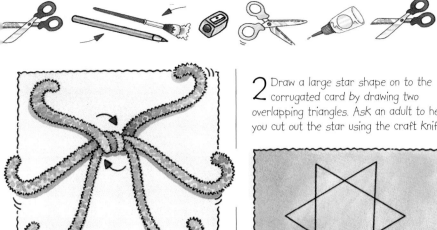

2 Draw a large star shape on to the corrugated card by drawing two overlapping triangles. Ask an adult to help you cut out the star using the craft knife.

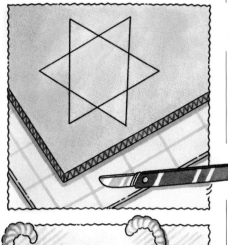

1 Take each pipe cleaner and bend both ends into a curly shape. Then firmly twist all the pipe cleaners together in the centre so they hold together and make the legs for the candle holder.

Make this beautiful candle holder to remind you of the light which Jesus brings.

3 Cover the pipe cleaners completely with several layers of glued strips of kitchen towel. This can get messy so cover the surface you are using with plenty of newspaper. Use the glue sparingly and let it dry in between layers.

4 Cover one side of the star with glued kitchen towel to give it a textured finish. Leave to dry, then cover the other side.

5 Place the star on a flat surface and position the pipe cleaners on top. Hold them in place with sticky tape and continue to apply the pieces of glued kitchen towel to secure the pipe cleaner legs firmly to the star. When the legs are dry they should be perfectly rigid and should support the star structure when turned the right way round.

6 Glue the lid to the centre of the star and cover with the glued kitchen towel. When you are happy that the candle holder is completely covered with the textured effect, leave to dry and paint it gold. Place the candle in the holder and wrap a small piece of tinsel or other small decorations around the centre of the holder.

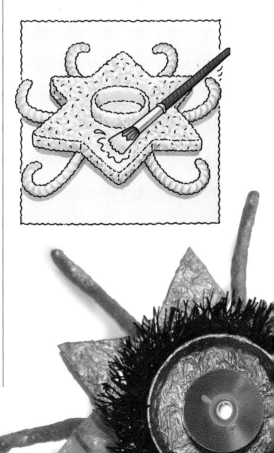

A NEW STAR IN THE SKY

The journey of the wise men

When Jesus was born, some wise men in the east were looking at the stars. They noticed a very bright new star in the sky and were very excited.

'Look at that!' said one of the wise men. 'A new king must have been born!'

So the wise men decided to set off to follow the star.

They took with them fine gifts for the new king.

They followed the star by day and by night, over deserts and hills.

Where would they find the king?

Use the star template shapes on pages 18 and 19 or draw your own star designs with a black felt tipped pen on to a sheet of white paper. When you place the coloured paper over the stars you will be able to see the outlines through the thin tissue.

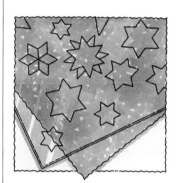

You will need:

Pack of coloured
tissue paper
or
coloured
hand-made papers

Gold or silver
relief fabric paint,
or
gold felt tipped
or glitter pens

Coloured A4 card

Scissors

Glue stick

Black
felt tipped pen
and white paper
(optional)

Plain ribbon
approximately
5cm wide

Use this star paper for your Christmas gifts.

2 Carefully trace the star shapes on to the paper with the gold pen or fabric paint. Trace as many stars as you can, drawing them all over the sheet. Draw a few test stars to see how long they take to dry. The paint must dry before moving on, otherwise the stars will smudge!

4 Overlap several pieces of torn paper to make your design. The papers are very thin so colours underneath will show through. Draw patterns and squiggles on the card with the gold pen to complete the design.

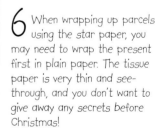

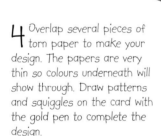

6 When wrapping up parcels using the star paper, you may need to wrap the present first in plain paper. The tissue paper is very thin and see-through, and you don't want to give away any secrets before Christmas!

3 To make a card, first fold a piece of coloured A4 card in half. Tear the paper around the star designs, leaving the uneven torn edges. Glue the back of the paper stars with the glue stick and stick them to the card. The paper is very delicate so use the glue stick carefully.

5 To make the gift tags, cut out small tag-size cards and decorate them as before. Also decorate the plain ribbon with stars and squiggles drawn with the glitter glue or fabric paint.

JEALOUS KING HEROD
Go to Bethlehem!

The star seemed to lead the wise men towards the great city of Jerusalem.

'Perhaps the new king has been born in the palace here,' said the wise men. So they knocked on the door of King Herod's palace.

'We have come to see the new king,' they said.

King Herod was a very jealous man. He wanted to be the only king around. He would have to get rid of this new king…

Herod called together the chief priests and teachers and asked them where the new king would be found.

'In Bethlehem,' they said.

'Go to Bethlehem and find the new king,' said Herod to the wise men. 'Then come back and tell me where to find him, so I too may go and worship him.'

You will need:

A4 sheets of coloured, holographic or patterned card

Scissors

PVA glue, brush, cocktail sticks

Thin wooden sticks

Acrylic paints and paint brush

Sparkly pipe cleaners, coloured feathers, stick-on gems and stars, stickers, sequins, ribbon, etc.

Coloured corrugated card

Shiny gold paper

Make these masks to act out the visit of the wise men to jealous King Herod.

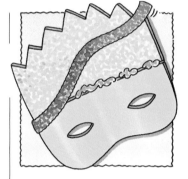

2 To make the crown mask, draw the crown shape on to gold holographic card and cut it out. Glue the crown in place on top of the eye mask, then glue a strip of glued ribbon over the join. Decorate the crown with sequins, stickers and tinsel.

3 To make the astronomer's mask, use the template to draw the turban shape on to patterned card, then cut it out. Glue the turban to the top of the eye mask and glue a strip of coloured corrugated card over the join.

1 Use the template on page 21 to draw the eye mask shape on to the card and cut out the mask with the scissors. To cut out the eyes, bend the card without creasing it and make a small snip in the middle of the eye with the tip of the scissors. Now you can get the scissors into the hole and cut out the eyes neatly. All the masks use this same eye mask shape.

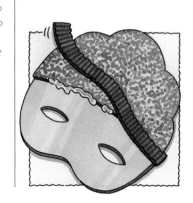

5 Make the other two masks in exactly the same way but decorate them differently. Use stick-on gems and stickers for one of the masks; glue coloured feathers under the centre decoration for the other design. Use whatever materials you have to decorate your masks.

6 Paint the wooden sticks with acrylic paints and decorate them with sequins or stickers, then glue them to the back of each mask. Leave the glue to dry before wearing the masks!

4 Cut some sparkly pipe cleaners into 10cm lengths and bend the ends over to make small hooks. Cut out sun, moon and star shapes from shiny gold paper or use stickers. Glue a shape to each of the curled ends of the pipe cleaners and leave to dry. Push the pipe cleaners into the corrugated slots and glue large shiny stars around the eye holes.

You will need:

✂

Some adult help with measuring and preparing the ingredients and utensils so everything is ready before you start!

Adult help with handling the tray of cookies in and out of the oven, preheated to 180°C/350°F or Gas mark 4

110g (4oz) butter

275g (10oz) plain flour

110g (4oz) brown sugar

1 teaspoon baking powder

75g (3oz) golden syrup

2 teaspoons ground ginger

1 medium egg

1 teaspoon cinnamon

110g (4oz) sifted icing sugar

1 tablespoon water

Food colours, silver balls and ribbon or cord for decoration

Wooden spoon and mixing bowl

Rolling pin

Greased baking tray

Wire cooling tray

Dessert spoon

Cookie cutters

Plastic straw

GIFTS FOR THE BABY KING

The wise men worship Jesus

The wise men set off towards Bethlehem. The star seemed to stop above a small house in the town.

They knocked on the door and went inside. There they found Mary, with Jesus on her knee. This was the new king they had travelled so far to see!

The wise men bowed down low and worshipped Jesus.

They gave him their fine gifts of gold, frankincense and myrrh. Mary watched in wonder.

God warned the wise men in a dream not to return to Herod's palace. And Joseph too was warned by God to take Mary and Jesus to Egypt, where they would be safe from cruel King Herod.

Make these delicious cookies to share at Christmas.

1 Cream the butter and sugar together in a bowl using the wooden spoon. Add the golden syrup and the egg, and mix until smooth.

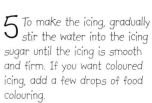

2 Sift the flour, baking powder and spices and fold them in to the mixture to form a stiff dough. Shape the dough into a ball and leave it in a cool place or the fridge for at least 1 hour.

3 Turn the dough on to a floured surface and roll out to 3mm thick. Use the cookie cutters to cut out the shapes and, using a plastic straw, make a hole in some of the cookies to hang on the tree. This quantity of dough will make approximately 8 large cookies plus 20 small ones.

4 Place the cookies on a greased baking tray and ask an adult to put them in a preheated oven to bake for 10-15 minutes, or until golden brown. Then leave them to cool on a wire tray.

5 To make the icing, gradually stir the water into the icing sugar until the icing is smooth and firm. If you want coloured icing, add a few drops of food colouring.

6 Decorate the cookies with the icing and silver balls and leave to dry. Thread ribbon through the holes of some of the cookies and hang them on the tree. The other cookies can be wrapped up and given as special Christmas presents or shared when visitors come.

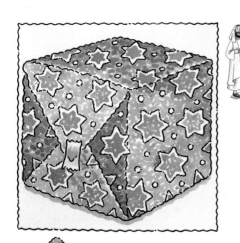

Where to find the stories in the Bible

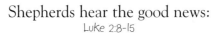

An angel visits Mary:
Luke 1:26-38

Mary and Joseph travel to Bethlehem:
Luke 2:1-5

Bethlehem is full:
Luke 2:1-7

Jesus is born:
Luke 2:6-7

Shepherds hear the good news:
Luke 2:8-15

Shepherds go to find Jesus:
Luke 2:16-20

Jesus is presented in the Temple:
Luke 2:21-38

A new star in the sky:
Matthew 2:1-2

Jealous King Herod:
Matthew 2:1-8

Gifts for the baby king:
Matthew 2:9-15

Published in the UK by
The Bible Reading Fellowship
First Floor, Elsfield Hall, 15-17 Elsfield Way,
Oxford OX2 8FG
ISBN 1 84101 350 1

First edition 2004

Editorial Director Annette Reynolds
Project Editor Leena Lane
Art Director Gerald Rogers
Pre-production Krystyna Hewitt
Production John Laister

British Library Cataloguing in Publication Data.
A catalogue record for this book is available
from the British Library.

Printed and bound in Singapore